ALL WHITE PEOPLE ARE NOT PRIVILEGED

MICHAEL D. MOSLEY

To order additional copies of this book, contact:
Xlibris
844-714-8691
www.Xlibris.com
Orders@Xlibris.com

ISBN: 978-1-6641-6905-0 (sc)
ISBN: 978-1-6641-6903-6 (hc)
ISBN: 978-1-6641-6904-3 (e)

Library of Congress Control Number: 2021907584

Print information available on the last page

Rev. date: 04/14/2021

DEDICATION

It is with great pleasure that I dedicate this book to Mr. Leo and Mrs. Peggy Ann Dugger. I know of no one who deserves it more. It was Aunt Peg and Uncle P-Joe who took me off that farm three or four summers as a little boy. I loved spending summers with them in Indianapolis. They treated me like I was their own. It was in their happy home that I got to see what love and happiness was all about. They loved each other so much. A week after I graduated high school, Aunt Peg was driving me all over Indianapolis to find a summer job. She found me a job downtown, and when I got my first paycheck, she and P-Joe refused to take any money. Not just anybody is willing to take on a hungry eighteen-year-old for free. They did. In the future, they would help both my brother and I find jobs again to help pay for college. She even found a house near hers so my mother, brother, and I could all work one summer in Indianapolis. We owe them so much for the sacrifices they made for us. I will always be grateful to them. This book is also dedicated to my mother Naomi Irene Mosley Littral.

This book tells the life story of a little boy who grows up in Appalachia, impoverished, and in a world where hope seems not to exist. The book starts as a biography but later morphs into an issue that America must tackle in the future to move forward. The issue is *inequality and injustice*. The author endorses the notion that all white people simply are not privileged. He embraces the attitude that "if you work hard, things will work out."

Ahead of you is a short autobiography. You must read the autobiography to understand where the author is coming from. During the summer of 2020, when several police officers killed black people, I too was outraged and angered at what was happening. Injustice and inequality are just wrong. However, many blacks in particular took this one step forward to conclude that "all white people are privileged." After reading the autobiography, you too will understand why this premise and thesis is wrong. All white people are *not* privileged. Read on.

1945: My story begins in Dayton, Ohio, when my sister Connie Jean was born on March 25, 1945, to my parents Naomi Irene Shepherd Mosley and Eldon Mosley. Mom was twenty, and Dad was thirty-five. She grew up in Whitesburg in Letcher Co, Kentucky, and he was from Manchester, Kentucky, in Clay Co. In 1945, World War II ended, and VP Harry S. Truman took over in Washington after Pres. Franklin D. Roosevelt died suddenly. Hitler committed suicide, and later that year, atomic bombs leveled Japan. Dachau concentration camp was liberated by American forces.

1946: My brother Ted Mosley was born on September 30, 1946, in Oneida, Kentucky (Clay County). My father named him after baseball great Ted Williams. Soldiers began coming home from the war, and the baby boom began. Gasoline cost 15¢ a gallon. The United Nations National Assembly held its first meeting. Sally Field, Dolly Parton, Donald Trump, and Ted Bundy were born this year. Assault won horse racing's Triple Crown, Saint Louis beat Boston in the World Series, and the Nuremburg Trials began in Germany. OKLA State beat UNC for the NCAA Championship.

1947: We lived in Ohio. Others who would call Ohio home include Grandmother Mallie L. Shepherd and her sisters Jean Shepherd Rowe and Jane Shepherd. Mom's brothers Bill and Jim lived their adult lives in Ohio and had successful careers in the insurance industry. In 1947, Jackie Robinson became the first black baseball player. The Cold War with Russia began. The Monroe Doctrine tried to rebuild Europe. Israel became a nation.

1948: I was born in Dayton, Ohio, on May 11, 1948. My father was a factory worker. My dear mother was at home with a newborn. Ted is two, and Connie is a curly-headed three-year-old. Four first cousins were also born this year: Diane Mosley, Geri Mosley, Bert Ison, and Bonnie Shepherd. I was born into a huge family. On my paternal side, I have my grandparents William and Margaret Noe Mosley and their six children: Aunt Pearl Mosley, Big Jim Mosley, Walker Mosley, Richard (Buster) Mosley, Orbin Mosley, and John D. Mosley. On the maternal side, I have Grandfather George Shepherd and Grandmother Mallie Hogg Shepherd and their ten children: George E. Shepherd, Jim Shepherd, Hubert Shepherd, Bill Shepherd, Bennie Joe Shepherd, Ray Shepherd, Jack Shepherd, Aunts Peggy and Maywood Shepherd, and of course, my mother Naomi Irene Shepherd. And large families like that was quite common in the '20s and '30s.

Also happening around the world: Prince Charles, Al Gore, Donna Summer, and Samuel L. Jackson were born in 1948. A loaf of bread was 14¢. Adolph Rupp coached Kentucky to its first NCAA Basketball Championship. Citation won the Kentucky Derby. Babe Ruth was laid to rest.

1949: This is a sad year. My grandfather George Shepherd, a former coal miner in Eastern Kentucky, died of lung disease (December 1948). He was laid to rest at the Pleasant View Cemetery, 5 miles west of London, Kentucky. My father Eldon was killed in a car and truck crash near Manchester, Kentucky. There were four men in the car. The driver (from Richmond) was booked into the Laurel County jail for driving under the influence. Another man was seriously injured and taken to Marymount Hospital in London. The other man was not seriously injured. Sadly, Eldon Mosley, my dad, suffered fatal injuries to the head and died at the scene. He was laid to rest at the Benge Cemetery in Clay County. Rominger Funeral Home in Manchester handled the services. My mother, who has a ninth grade education and no skills, was now left with three small children to raise. The factory where my father worked covered its employees with life insurance, and a small amount of money was awarded to my mother. It was at this time that Bill and Ruth Shepherd took our small family in to help us. We lived with them briefly. In 1949, homes cost $7,450. Berlin was blockaded this year. George Orwell wrote *1984*. NATO was established. The first Volkswagen Beetle was made. The NBA was born. Lionel Richie, Jessica Lange, and Bruce Springsteen were born. Kentucky defeated Oklahoma A&M to win its second NCAA Championship. Americans started to buy televisions.

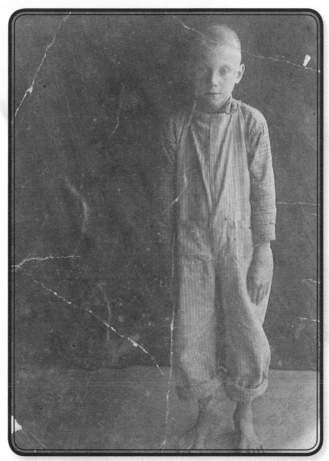

Eldon Mosley
1910-1949

1950: Mom was twenty-five, Connie was 5, Teddy (often called that) was three, and Mikie was coming out of diapers at age two. These were postwar years, and these were very hard times. We thanked Bill and Ruth, and we moved on to our own place. Coming from a large family pays off as they all chipped in to help our little family. Auntie Jean bought my sister a tricycle. My mother pondered over whether she wanted to raise her children in city housing or possibly purchase a small farm in Kentucky, where other relatives lived, in Laurel and Clay Counties, Kentucky. My mother decided to purchase a very small farm, 6 miles west of London, Kentucky, on Route 1, Road 192, a dirt road. The farm consisted a small two-room house and a smokehouse in the back. This farm included a barn, a pond, and enough land to have a vegetable garden and a small tobacco patch. There was no indoor plumbing. It was about this time that my mother met and wedded a man from this community (Cold Hill), and his name was Ledford Anders.

Fresh out of the army, he had no particular skills and was a lazy farmer. He loved my mother, but us kids, not so much! So we were a family of five now, living in near poverty. We referred to this house as the little house.

Elsewhere in 1950: The Korean War was heating up. working wages per year were $3,210. The people of Guam were granted US citizenship. Favorite movies of that year were *"Annie Get Your Gun,"* and *"Sunset Boulevard,"* and Middleground won the Kentucky Derby. The NCAA Tournament, consisting of eight teams, was won by CCNY as they knocked off Bradley.

In The Beginning

Connie – Ted – Mike

Mommy – Ted – Connie

3 year old Mike

GROWING UP IN KENTUCKY

The Home Place – The 2 Room School House

1951: My sister turned six years old this year and headed off to Cold Hill Grade School for first grade. Kindergarten did not exist. This was a two-room schoolhouse with no cafeteria and no indoor plumbing. Children brought their lunch in a small lard tin can, and most were filled with peanut butter and crackers. Ted and I were at home with Mom, while our stepfather worked well-drilling jobs. We were surrounded with good neighbors: the Browns, Byrd, and Smith families. Life was simple. We had no phone, TV, or indoor plumbing, but we were reasonably happy. We did have radio, and we listened to WFTG in London and WCTT in Corbin, which carried all University of Kentucky Wildcats basketball games. Occasionally, we would walk back to the house of the Byrd family (Barbara, Dean, and Ruth Ann) and watched their new TV, which was black and white, of course. At 4:00 p.m., we were all glued to the TV to watch *Howdy Doody* and Pinky Lee with Clarabelle the clown. And yes, in summertime, we did, in fact, go *barefooted*. A large washtub could be found in the backyard, where we bathed. In 1951, *I Love Lucy* came to TV, and the best movies were *The African Queen* and *A Streetcar Named Desire*. UK beat Kansas State for their third national championship.

1952: Connie began second grade, and Ted entered first grade at Cold Hill School. I was four years old and at home with Mom. Laurel County has a dozen of these small grade schools with their "pot belly stoves." Wyan and Cold Hill had two rooms, referred to as the little room (grades 1–4) and the big room (grades 5–8), and paddling was certainly allowed. Harold Reams was a frequent flyer. Teachers were not required to have a BS in Education; two years at Sue Bennett Junior College would get you hired. It wasn't until around 1970 that LCPS would consolidate and upgrade its schools and standards. Mom and I would take long walks as we had the world to ourselves. We'd have long talks with Lonnie Irving and his wife, as well as Florie Smith. Mom would say, "Now doesn't he look just like me?" The mop of blond hair, big blue eyes, and puffy lips were a dead giveaway. I enjoyed this year as I had her all to myself. Postwar America was changing. In 1952, the *NBC Today* show debuted, *The Diary of a Young Girl* by Anne Frank was published, Nelson Mandela was jailed, and a new car cost $1,700. Nearly fifty thousand American children were struck with the polio pandemic. Queen Elizabeth II was crowned and amazingly sits on the throne today. The Summer Olympics resumed in Helsinki. KFC began in Corbin, Kentucky. Sharon Osborne and Christopher Reeve were born. Hill Gail took the Derby, and Kansas beat Saint Johns in the NCAA Finals.

1953: Tragedy visited again. Mom's younger brother, Bennie Joe Shepherd (Airman 2nd Class USAF), hopped a B-25 from Florida to Andrews AFB in DC. He was headed to Dayton to visit family and his girlfriend. The plane with five airmen left Florida and flew into a bad rainstorm in SW Georgia (Pine Mountain, just north of Warm Springs). The plane crashed into the mountain. The heavy rain prevented a fire, but the crash killed the crew. Locals, including a minister, rushed up the mountain. They found the crash and my young uncle. The minister prayed fervently as Uncle Bennie Joe breathed his last breath. Somehow one airman survived. Our family was devastated. In 1953, it was customary for the deceased to be brought to the family home. And so House Funeral Home in London draped a large maroon curtain on the western wall of my grandmother's house. The casket with its glass covering was brought into the room. His mother and nine brothers and sisters gathered around. It was the most heartbreaking thing I had ever seen. I saw my handsome young uncle for the first and last time. Three days later, the funeral and burial were concluded with full military honors. In just five years, my mother had now lost her husband, her father, and her young brother. Grief filled our home.

This photo was taken shortly after the funeral of my Uncle Bennie Joe Shepherd. In this picture, Grandmother Shepherd is holding the folded frag from the Casket. Present are all his siblings, Maywood, Peggy, Jim Hubert, George E., Naomi, Bill, Jack and Ray

1954: We moved forward, living in the little house, and all three of us kids attended Cold Hill, and I (six years old) was in the first grade class of Mrs. Emma Burns. She quickly taught us, "If you need to go out to the toilet, put up your hand with *one* finger up to go 'wee wee and *two* fingers up for the other." Months later, I fling up my hand with *two* fingers waving vigorously. She continued teaching the second graders. I waved frantically. Finally, she saw the urgency in my blue face! I raced to the door and trotted quickly to the outdoor toilet. Dear Lord, I did not make it. It slid down my britches, and I began to cry. How would I ever go back into the school room with that odor? After thirty minutes, I cleaned myself as much as I could, dried my eyes, and slithered back into the classroom. Heads turned! Small kids grabbed their noses. Within a minute, the odor backed Mrs. Burns up against the chalkboard. She called a *quick recess*. The room cleared in two seconds. Since it was a sunny fall day and the weather was warm, she asked me to sit on the school steps for the final twenty minutes of the school day. *She never made that mistake again!* Little Mikie Mosley would be allowed to relieve himself at the first hint.

Elsewhere in 1954: Dwight Eisenhower was president. Sen. Joe McCarthy was censured. We watched *Father Knows Best* on TV. The Supreme Courts said "Separate but equal" is inherently unequal. The popular movies were *Seven Brides for Seven Brothers* and *On the Waterfront*. John Travolta was born. LaSalle won the NCAA Tournament. The NY Giants took the World Series over the Indians in a 4-0 sweep.

NOTE: A hint of bad times to come. My stepfather and mother got into a serious argument, and he struck her in the mouth, chipping her front teeth. She grabbed up her three kids and walked a mile to her mother's farmhouse (referred to as the big white house). We spent the night there. "Real men do not hit women," I said to myself.

The Grade School Days – Mike and Ted Mosley

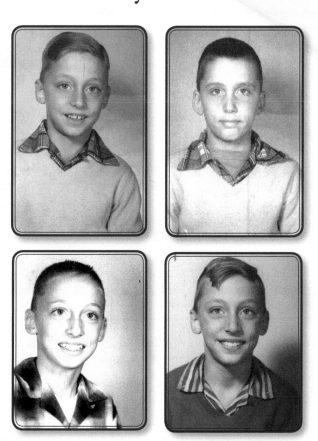

1955: Big changes were coming. My grandmother decided that she and the last of her brood (Jackie Lee and Ray) would move into town where she took a job at the hospital. This opened the door for us to move from the little house to the big white house and the huge farm. The farm was over 200 acres and had lots of cattle and was actually owned by my uncle George, who was a major in the US Marines. We changed schools. Connie was a fifth grader, Ted was in third grade, and I was in second grade at Wyan Grade School. Ledford tried his hand at big-time farming (cattle and tobacco). My mother got a job at the state TB hospital in town. She rode to work with Marie Alsip, another nurse aide. Tobacco farmers lived for December, when they take their tobacco to market. Everybody in the family worked long hard days. At Christmas, I walked a mile back into our farm and cut down a 5-foot cedar tree (Christmas tree) that would fit into a water bucket filled with gravels to hold the tree up. Santa brought us a bike, but of course, Ted and I must share it. Mama said, "Poor people do as poor people can." We finally purchased a TV and had a phone put into the farmhouse. Of course, we were on a party line and must wait until neighbor Lucy Killion finishes her endless gossip hour before we could call cousin Chuck up and invite him over. The '50s, for me, was the "age of innocence." We roamed all over the huge farm and countryside, camping out, swimming in our own pond, climbing in our apple orchard, listening to the World Series, pickin' strawberries for Mr. Wyan, walking to the country store for a pop, riding with Dink and Dorie Greer to Hart Baptist Church, going to the Reda Theater to watch westerns with Sonny Ray Hale. Yes, it was a good time for a little boy to grow up.

Around the world: The Salk vaccine was introduced to combat polio. James Dean starred in *East of Eden*. Elvis Presley hit the stage. Seat belts were invented. The Mickey Mouse Club opened. Walt Disney opened Disneyland California. McDonald's opened. The top movie was *Rebel Without a Cause*. The Brooklyn Dodgers won the World Series, and the San Francisco Dons won the 1955 NCAA Basketball Tournament.

1956: In the third grade talent show, I entered myself as Elvis, stepped in front of the class, and sang and danced just like him. Mrs. Hazel Johnson, our teacher was not amused. The class went wild. I was an instant hit with my classmates. Ted was in fourth grade, and Connie was on the other side of the folding doors in the big room (sixth grade). Work on the farm became harder as stepfather Ledford had become more difficult to please, and we began finding whiskey bottles hidden around the house. Mom worked hard at making the marriage work by having family cookouts and playing croquet and badminton with us. At Christmas, these two-room schoolhouses had a tradition that warms the heart. The teacher gives every student a brown bag full of goodies. An orange, an apple, a huge stick of hard candy, and nuts filled the bag and was given out on the last day of school before Christmas break. We had a Christmas play some years. We sang carols and decorated a tree with homemade decorations. The Bradley girls always brought plenty popcorn for all to enjoy. Those Kentucky winters were very cold, but we loved the snow. We'd listen to the radio at 6:00 a.m., hoping to hear, "Laurel County Schools are closed today." That meant sledding, building snowmen, finding a shallow puddle covered by ice, and skating. Country kids can always find a way to amuse themselves. Ted and I put a basketball hoop up inside an old vacant farmhouse and had our own "Memorial Coliseum." Also happening in 1956: Winter Olympics were in Cortina, Italy. Americans built 41,000 miles of interstate roads. *As the World Turns* was the number one soap. The best movie was *The Ten Commandments*. Khruschev came to power in USSR. Grace Kelly married Prince Rainier III of Monaco. Fifty-two people were killed when the "SS *Andrea Doria* and MS *Stockholm*" collided. Eisenhower defeated Stevenson, the SF Dons won in the NCAA, and the Yankees beat the Dodgers in the World Series.

1957: Tommy Ray Smith and I (fourth graders, no less) had run around the schoolyard, yelling, "I like *Ike*!" And it seems to have paid off. Eisenhower took office in January after having suffered a heart attack that had put him in the hospital for three weeks. Looks like having a TV paid off. Wyan School—oh, the memories! Our lunchroom cook, Myrtle Wyan, could make the best grilled cheese in all the world. We paid 50¢ a week for lunches that were delicious. It was about this time in my life that my aunt Peg would invite me to come to Indianapolis with her and husband P-Joe for three or four weeks in the summer. We ate lots of White Castle burgers and went to the drive-in theater every Friday night. They took me to Riverside Amusement Park each visit, and I'd ride the Wild Mouse roller coaster, and later I'd hurl all the cotton candy. Life was grand as a nine-year-old, where there was peace and tranquility in the house. I am grateful to them for all they did for me. Years later, I would return to Naptown and work my way through college, thanks to Aunt Peg. When the summer with them in Indianapolis was over, I'd ride a Greyhound bus home to Kentucky.

Elsewhere in 1957: A dozen eggs cost 28¢. New tv shows were *Perry Mason* and *Maverick*. Frisbees and Hula-Hoops were the latest craze. Seventy thousand Americans died of Asian flu. Hurricane Audrey killed five hundred in the South. Nine blacks enrolled at previously segregated Little Rock Central High. The best movie was *Bridge over River Quai*. Donnie Osmond and Gloria Estefan were born. UNC won the NCAA, and the Milwaukee Braves beat NY in the World Series.

My Sister Connie

1958: This one year, Connie (eighth grade), Ted (sixth grade), and I (fifth grade) would all be in the same classroom. Our cousin Diane Mosley was also in this room. We had the most wonderful teacher in Mrs. Kathleen Pope. She had thirty students in four grades, all in one room. We played a mean game of softball, and some of our best Wyan players were Glen and Joe Pope, Polly and Janet Wyan, Ted Mosley, Roy Philpot, the Sparkmans and Bradleys, and many others. We'd play Cold Hill School and also New Sharon School. Mrs. Pope would let Ted and her son Joe go outside and listen to the World Series games, with the promise that they would come back into the class and tell us what was happening. We were old enough now to notice cars. Cars in this day and age had big fins, and they were huge. We made fun of Edsels and Studebakers. Connie was crowned the 4-H Queen for Wyan School. Mom purchased a beautiful $40 pink formal prom dress, and off we went to the London Junior High Cafeteria for the county competition. I am proud to tell you my sister Connie, who looked fifteen, took second place to Judy Harkleroad. We drove home very proud of her.

"Forty dollars for a damn dress!" the mean stepfather screamed. "Are you crazy?"

Things at home were not going well, and I could see that our parents would be separating. Over the next two years, we did, in fact, move out several times and found a places to rent. Sadly, we returned. These moves happened so many times, we can hardly name them all now, as we are all in our seventies.

Around the world: A famine hit China. The Russian *Sputnik* was launched. Toyota and Datsun hit the American market. Rockefeller was governor of New York. The first Boeing 707 was rolled out. John XXIII was pope. *Vertigo* was the top movie. Tanya Tucker and Jamie Lee Curtis were born. Kentucky won the NCAA over Seattle, and the Yankees won the '58 World Series over Milwaukee.

NOTE: As I talk about moving a lot and changing schools, please keep in mind how resilient children are. I learned this in my master's program at WKU many years later. But we three children lived this "resiliency" in the late '50s and early '60s. We did move often. We came to accept it and made the best of it.

1959: (Connie, ninth grade, HGHS; Ted, seventh grade, Wyan; Mike, sixth grade, Wyan) Since the three of us start changing schools over the next few school years, I feel the need to get the events in order. Bear with me. Connie Jean would ride the Harvey Lawson Bus 29 to Hazel Green High. Ted and I were still at Wyan. Often was the case, that Harvey would pull up in front of our house and lay down on the *horn*. Eventually, she would come running out of the house. Books, papers, and makeup flying in all directions., and it was all so predictable. This would be the year Ted, Chuck, Sonny Hale, Tommy Smith, and yours truly would come up with a great idea: THE PARADISE CLUB. The club, a converted smokehouse, was located just behind our farm home. Since we no longer hung salted meat there, it was basically a large storage room. It had a few old mattresses in it too. So we invited all the neighbor boys to come join our club. Of course, Ted proclaimed himself president. (The club would *not* be based on democracy.) It was a great place for a sleepover. We'd borrow our sister's record player and all her 45s (music on plastic) and play them *loud*. We were preteens, so we'd have to talk about all the pretty girls in the neighborhood and who we might date someday. Not long after that, we came up with "The Great Pinkney Wyan Melon Heist." Pinkney was a neighbor who grew the sweetest watermelons in all the county. We decided that on a Saturday night, around midnight, we would slither through the woods with coffee sacks, crawl down the rows of ripe melons, pluck the best, and crawl back out with a dozen or so melons. However, Mr. Wyan woke up, heard some noise in his melon patch, grabbed his gun, and shot in the air. Thankfully, he missed everything. I ran straight into a tree. Sonny screamed that a snake had bitten him. Scared out of our wits, we grabbed our coffee sacks with several good melons and headed for the woods where we would hike a mile to a designated place and eat the melons. We dug a hole and put the remaining melons in it and returned each afternoon after school to laugh, eat watermelon, and talk about how cool the whole adventure had been. Boys will be boys. Around the world in 1959: Castro came to power in Cuba. Alaska and Hawaii became states. The price of a movie was 50¢. The best movies were *Ben-Hur* and *Sound of Music*. New TV shows were *The Twilight Zone* and *Bonanza*. Barbie was a big hit. The LA Dodgers beat Chicago White Sox in '59 Series, and California beat West Virginia in the NCAA Finals.

1960: (Connie, tenth grade, London High; Ted, eighth grade, London Junior High; Mike, seventh grade, London Junior High) We are living in town now. Ted and I were on the top floor of London Elementary, which housed the seventh and eighth graders, where the teachers rotate classrooms all day. I was in Mrs. Kidd's room. I find schoolwork more challenging and the students better prepared than the two-room school setting. For the first time ever, I had homework, and I learned to study. I was elected president of my class. I was shocked and surprised. We had a French teacher a few times a month and a physical education teacher (Mr. Hendrix) for the first time in my schooling. Living in town was fun too. I loved living close to the Reda Theater, Hoskin's 5&10 and a great assortment of chocolates, walking to LHS football and basketball games, skating at the Ray Reams Rink, playing basketball at Mill Street Park and Barton's court, and hanging out with Ronnie Ingram. I had a friend named Rodney Gunnell, and his mother worked alongside my mom at the TB Hospital. Sadly, she succumbed to cancer that year. Ted and I went out for football. I was assigned a uniform and hit the field for practice. I was the smallest kid there. In a real time practice that week, Richard Riley, a running back who weighed twice my weight, did an end around and was heading straight toward me. I prayed, "Lord, he is going to *kill* me." He weighed 180 lbs., and I weighed maybe 75 lbs. He was running full speed and hit me full on. I saw stars, my helmet was now on backward, I hurt all over, and trainers ran to me. Riley was in the endzone in a flash. I was carried to the sideline, where I stayed the rest of the practice. After practice, Coach Kuhl/Woolum talked to me. "Maybe, when you have put on a bit more weight, you can try out again." It was a relief to hear those words, and I never put on a football uniform again in my life. Ted was bigger and faster, and he stayed on and actually got to dress out for the Harlan Rosenwald High game. We had the choice of walking home for lunch or eating in the cafeteria. We shared a can of Campbell's Soup. To this day, I cannot look at canned soup as I shop at Publix. In the spring, we seventh and eighth graders put on a folk dance festival in the gym for parents and community. It was sold out. We did every kind of dance you could think of, including the cuckoo waltz. My dance partner Sue Peace still had sores on her feet from the trampling I gave her that night. But my mother and grandmother were there, and I was proud when it was over. I still can hear Mr. Hendrix yelling at me in practice, "The other *left* foot, Mosley." Toward the end of the year, I was diagnosed with "histoplasmosis" and sent home for a month of bedrest. I barely passed seventh grade. By 1960, my mother had decided that her marriage might never work out.

Around the world in 1960: JFK was elected. Coke in cans came out. Gas was 25¢ a gallon. *To Kill a Mocking Bird* was published. Cassius Clay (Muhammad Ali) won the gold in Rome. The best movie was *Psycho* by Hitchcock. Pirates beat NY Yankees in the World Series, and Ohio State won the NCAA Championship.

1961: (Connie, eleventh grade, HGHS; Ted, ninth grade, HGHS; Mike, eighth grade, Wyan). Connie and Ted were now riding the bus to Hazel Green High. I was finishing up my elementary year at Wyan. We talked Ted and Roy Pope into helping us form a basketball team at Wyan, complete with uniforms, practice sessions, and a short schedule. London Junior High was happy to schedule us as they knew we were an upstart team and a sure victory. So the Wyan Hornets showed up at the London High School Gym. None of us had ever played a game "indoors." The bright lights, real refs in stripes, and huge floor quickly humbled and confused us. Our center, Tommy Smith, got confused (having only played on a half court) and put the ball back up and in the basket—on the wrong basket. Two points for the London Tigers. I'll get right to the finish—it was a long and ugly game. We lost by twenty. At Hazel Green, Ted went out for basketball and made the B team. Connie was a jolly junior and had her eyes on basketball star Alvin Tuttle. Connie and I were allowed to go skating on Saturday nights, but Mom whispered in my ear, "She is not allowed to sit in cars with boys who flirt with her." I was a wimpy kid, but I kept an eye on my big sister who had grown into a "real looker." Meanwhile, Ledford had been conned into building a prefab house in Leeds County, with the hopes of getting us to move back to the country. We did come back briefly, only to find the house was only half completed, and Ledford used us as free labor to finish the place. Next, Mom moved us to a house on US 80, next door to Ted's best friend Larry Onkst. Mom was driving me to Wyan early one winter morning, and she hit black ice, and the car spun around and around before stopping at the edge of a cliff with a 50-foot drop-off. We said a quick prayer of thanks for the skinny tree that held the car from going over. We move to Sublimity. I rode my bike to school, problem solved.

Around the world in 1961: Russian Yuri Gagarin was the first man in space. The Berlin Wall went up. Kennedy's "Bay of Pigs" attempt to overthrow Castro failed. The Peace Corps was born. We danced the pony and twist. Popular TV shows were *Wagon Train*, *Andy Griffith Show*, and *Gunsmoke*. George Clooney and Barack Obama were born. Yankees beat Reds in WS, and Cincinnati beat Ohio State in NCAA Finals.

1962: (Connie, twelfth grade, HGHS; Ted, tenth grade, HGHS; Mike, ninth grade, HGHS; Mom, LPN) Mom took the licensed practical nurse test and passed. We were proud of her, and this meant more income. Connie began her senior year at HGHS, where both Ted and I were also attending. We walked to Begley Drug to catch the old faithful Harvey Lawson's crazy bus no. 29. I say that because it was a long wild ride with warnings from Harvey, like "Wes Harville, put that cigarette out!" Later my first report card was handed to me by Coach Reed who said to us in homeroom, "Now, boys, this is the kind of report card you should all strive for." It was straight As. I was proud, but it never happened again. Connie entered the talent show and did a great imitation of Mrs. Tankersley, her English teacher. Ted was on the B team, and Coach Sam Karr was building a great era of basketball at Hazel Green High. The Bullfrogs made it to the twelve-region championship in 1962, where it was once again played at Somerset High. Somerset won. But that was not the major event in our lives in 1962. A great deal happened in 1962. Although we were not living with Ledford Anders, we were shocked to learn that he had died of an accident at the age of forty-two. The cause of death was a broken neck after a fall over a ditch. Alcohol was involved. We attended the funeral. Mom was pretty shaken up. They were not divorced. Time marched on. A tobacco buyer from Mullins, South Carolina, met and distracted my mother from her loneliness. They fell in love, but later we found out he was married (his wife was an invalid). Connie dated and fell for a redheaded lab technician from the hospital. Ted swooned for a girl down the road named Elaine. My god! Our house had turned into *Peyton Place*. Meanwhile, just 90 miles from Miami, the Russians were placing missiles in Cuba. JFK called their bluff, and the Russians backed down. John Glenn orbited the earth. While the Beatles sang "Love Me do," Marilyn Monroe sang "Happy Birthday, Mr. President." Walmart and Kmart opened. The best movies were *Lawrence of Arabia* and *West Side Story*. Jodi Foster was born. And in sports, the Cincy Bearcats met and beat Ohio State *again* in the NCAA Finals, while the Yankees took down the SF Giants in World Series play.

1963: (Connie got married; Ted, eleventh grade, HGHS; Mike, tenth grade, London High). Connie and John Sherry Bentley were married now. Shocker! Mom purchased a new "manufactured home," and we moved to Mill Street in London. It was very modern and clean. Ted caught the bus to Hazel Green at the Sonoco Station, and I decided to transfer to London High, since we live a half mile from the school. No more wild bus rides for me. I had very challenging teachers. Mrs. Emily B. Tucker was my tenth grade world history teacher. She could make the Austro-Hungarian empire and the Hapsburgs come alive. Ted, cousin Chuck, and I were being taught driver education by an old family friend Dick Gunnell. We drove around the local teen hangouts: Finley's, Dairy Dart, and Bruners. We made weekend trips to the Cumberland Gap, Cudjo's Cave, and the Corbin bowling alley. We were typical teenagers. We religiously followed the Cincinnati Reds, UK Wildcats, and twelve-region basketball. Ted was moved to the varsity at Hazel Green High, and we paid close attention to the sports pages. The first grandchild in our family (Sheri Jean) was born. Everybody remembers 1963. Pres. John F. Kennedy was assassinated in Dallas. After taking a walk across the hall from the principal's office, our sixth period world history teacher, Mrs. Tucker, walked back into class. Tears flowed as she said, "The president has been shot dead in Dallas, Texas." The world stopped briefly as we caught our breaths. That weekend we were glued to the TV. Nothing prepares you for horrific events in life like this. People looked for answers. There were none. Sadly, this would not be the last time great people are shot down. The world mourned with America.

Elsewhere in 1963: The average American made $5,807. Alcatraz prison was closed. Beatlemania began. The post office launched zip codes. The first American Express Card was mailed out. Pope John XXIII died. MLK delivered "I Have a Dream" speech. Favorite TV shows were *Mr. Ed* and *The Flintstones*. Michael Jordan was born. LA Dodgers beat the Yankees in WS, and Loyola of Chicago beat Cincy in the 1963 NCAA Championship game in overtime.

1964–1965: (Connie, cosmetology school; Ted, senior, HGHS; Mike, junior, London High) Connie and her husband Sherry lived in Richmond briefly while he attended EKU. By 1965, they were headed to Lexington. Meanwhile, back in London, Mom got her ten-year pin at the hospital, and Ted entered his senior year at Hazel Green High, where he started most basketball games. This was a banner year for the Bullfrog basketball team. Ted and I had been working for a couple of years now for Atty. Calvert "Red" Little, a man who many said was destined to be governor of Kentucky. We cleaned his office once a week. On weekends, we cleaned the family pool and mowed the massive lawn; Ted on a riding mower and me behind a push mower, of course. If you want spending money and snazzy clothes, you must be willing to work for it. My brother and I were close even though we attend rival high schools. I pulled for his team, except when they were playing my London Tigers. As luck would have it, both teams made it to the twelve-region basketball championship game in Danville, Kentucky. Both teams were ranked in Kentucky's top 20. The game was going my way. With two minutes to play, London High had a five-point lead, and our fans were already chanting, "On to State!" All of a sudden, Coach Karr put Ted in the game. The only three shots my brother took that night were dead on, and the Hazel Green fans went wild. They won the game by one point, and my brother was named, forevermore, "Three Shot Mosley." This left me standing in the middle of the LHS crowd, totally conflicted. On the one hand, I was so happy my very own brother was the hero of the tournament. At the same time, I looked around, and my London classmates were in tears. It was the worst of times and the best of times. When we get home from the two-hour drive through Crab Orchard, we replayed the game over and over. The celebration was cut short. The very next day, our Grandmother Shepherd passed away. Connie was in the same hospital, having her second child. Our emotions were on a roller coaster. At State, Hazel Green made it all the way to the final four but fell to the Holy Cross Indians at Freedom Hall in Louisville with thirteen thousand in attendance. In the fall of 1965, Ted was given a full basketball scholarship to Sue Bennett Junior College, right there in London. The NCAA Champion in '64 was UCLA and again in 1965.

NOTE: It was about this time that our uncle Ray took us to UK football and basketball games. Uncles Bill, Ray, and George began counseling us as to the values of a college education. They preached long and hard and told us to major in business or accounting. I did not have the heart to tell them I had just finished taking accounting in high school with a final grade of D. We owed it to these three uncles and our dear mother that Ted and I both finished well above the master's degree.

1965—1966: (Connie, Lexington; Ted, freshman at SBC; Mike, senior, LHS) My senior year at London High finally rolled around. We lived at the Calvert Little Apartments, which had just been built. Ted walked to school at Sue Bennett Junior College and got a rude awakening to college level courses. They had a good team at SBC, and I attended most of his games. Connie and John lived in Lexington, and they visited often, and we spoiled those two tiny girls. I took psychology and sat beside my cousin Bert Ison, and our teacher was Jerry Brown. I really enjoyed this course. I have always said the seed was laid in that high school psych class for my masters in counseling and psychology. But that came later. Basketball tournament rolled around, and once again, London High was ranked 13 in the state, but sadly, we fell to the Lily Bulldogs in the district tournament, first round. More heartbreak for the Tiger fans. I had a few dates that year and took Arlene Burnette to the prom in May. We are friends to this date. A growth spurt moved me all the way from 5-foot-8 to 5-foot-11. I could now give my brother and cousin Chuck a good game of basketball at Mill Street Park. I graduated in May 1966, and a week later, I was in Indianapolis, where my wonderful Aunt Peg helped me find a summer job. My goal was to attend Sue Bennett Junior College in the fall. She helped me find a factory job Downtown Indianapolis. I rode the city bus to work and back. I even rode the bus downtown once to hear Pres. Lyndon Johnson make a speech on the circle. Out of the kindness of their hearts, Aunt Peg and Uncle P-Joe charged me absolutely nothing, so I was able to save everything I made. And it would be needed as fall semester rolled around, and I joined my brother at SBC, about ten blocks from home. My college teachers were outstanding, and I made a 2.80 during my first semester. Luckily, that was exactly what I needed to earn the "Methodist Scholarship," which would tide me over for second semester.

Around the world in 1966: The miniskirt became fashionable. Troops were sent to Vietnam. The population of the United States was 195 million. America started to experience mass murders, like the Richard Speck murder of eight nurses in Chicago and the University of Texas tower shooting that killed fourteen. Race riots broke out in Atlanta and around the United States. The top movie was *Dr. Zhivago* and Who' Afraid of Virginia Wolf. The Mamas & the Papas entertain us with "Monday, Monday," and the Orioles sweep the Dodgers in the WS. This would not be a typical NCAA Tournament. In 1966, Kentucky would meet Texas Western (now UTEP) for the championship. Tex. Western started five blacks, and UK from the SEC was all white. Don Haskins coached Texas Western to a 72-65 win as a shocked world watched on national TV. This would be a historic game, and after this game, Coach Rupp and all SEC schools started recruiting black athletes.

1966–1967 (Connie and John, Lexington; Ted, sophomore, SBC; Mike, freshman, SBC) My year at Sue Bennett was a fun one. I dated a girl named Janet from Missouri. She and I double-dated with Ronnie Ingram and Reba Hampton. Ted was now captain of the Sue Bennett Junior College basketball team, in his second year there, and was also named Mr. Acropolis (Mr. Sue Bennett). I want to share a story about one of his games so you will know it is the 1960s.

The team and Coach Wiggins traveled in a small bus from Kentucky to South Georgia to take on Brewton Parker Junior College. Shortly after passing Macon, they stopped in a small town to eat. (Remember, the team was mixed with black and white players). Strangely, the coach picked a restaurant, and he said, "Stay on the bus, I'll be right back."

The owner of the restaurant saw that there were blacks on the bus. He told Coach Wiggins, "Move on down the road. We do not serve niggahs here."

Coach returned to the bus, and they moved on. The white players were puzzled. "Why are we not eating?"

The black players knew exactly what just went down. The black players quietly enlightened the white boys. "It happens all the time down here but not in Kentucky," they said.

By now, President Johnson had signed into law several civil rights acts. Deep Southerners ignore them. They eventually found a place to eat, and later on they won the game, thanks to Hot-Shot Thompson. Ted and I finished up at Sue Bennett Junior, and when he started planning his transfer to EKU, I too made the move. We worked one summer at a box factory in Indianapolis. The next two summers, we worked our way through college by working at the US Army Ammunition Plant in Charlestown, Indiana, and Mom got nursing jobs in nursing homes. It was not until many years later that I realized what a sacrifice my mother had made for us boys. She wanted us to have what she did not have—a college education.

Around the world in 1967: UCLA owned the NCAA. The first Super Bowl was played. The minimum wage was $1.40. The United States sent 475,000 more soldiers to Vietnam. Israel won the six-day war with Arabs. Expo '67 took place in Montreal. *Rolling Stone* magazine debuted. Ali refused military service. Forty thousand gathered in San Francisco to protest the war. Presley married Priscilla. Otis Redding died in a place crash. TV favorites were *Bewitched*, *The Beverly Hillbillies*, *General Hospital*, and *Hogan's Heroes*.

1967–1968: (Connie and John now had three kids; Ted, junior, EKU; Mike, sophomore, EKU-MSU; Mom, Indianapolis) We settled into living on a campus with seventeen thousand students. Ted was in Commonwealth Hall, and I was in Palmer Hall, next door. It's fun to walk to football and basketball games in the new Alumni Coliseum. EKU battled WKU to a 14-14 tie in football at Hanger Field. Food and dances at the Keene Student Center were a short walk away. There were over fifty students from our hometown of London attending the university, and we ran into them often. My roomie is a nutjob from Barbourville. Ted and Joe from Somerset settled in. Greek mythology was my hardest course, and I spent long hours in my room reading *Oedipus Rex*, while my brother struggled through history of the Western civilization with Dr. Cedric Yo. Before long, I was informed that some of my courses at SBC were not accepted, although Ted's were. We got into a heated argument. It dragged on, and I informed the university that I planned to transfer to Morehead State, where all credits at Sue Bennett were fully accepted. After Christmas break, I did, in fact, made the move to Morehead State, 90 miles away. I had my own room and used it to study the *most difficult* course I would ever take, Invertebrate Zoology. I made friends with a guy next door from Danville. Wendell Ford Hall was now home. Al and I walked over to Laughlin Fieldhouse to watch the best team in the Ohio Valley Conference. Hobo Jackson and Lamar Green had the seven-thousand-seat fieldhouse full of screaming fans every game. Oddly, the president's wife, Mrs. Adrian Doran, played the organ at timeouts, piped directly into the fieldhouse, and the packed crowd stood and sang, "Fight, fight, fight for Morehead State." It was so loud, the opponents could not hear anything in the huddle. I loved Morehead, but like most of their mountain-area students, I too was very poor, so poor I went to

Pasquale's Restaurant to eat and had to write a cold check to pay for my meal. The owner would wink at me as he knew I would make good on the check next week. And I did as Mom sent a care package. In the spring of 1968, Martin Luther King was shot and killed in Memphis. These were turbulent times. Western Kentucky won the OVC in '67 and Murray State in '68. UCLA won the NCAA '67 and '68. Boring.

1969–1972: (Connie and Mom, Lexington; Ted, first Mosley to graduate college; Mike, senior, EKU) In the fall of 1968, EKU reversed itself and accepted all credits, and I returned for my junior year. My brother graduates EKU in '69 and became the first Mosley to earn a college degree. He married Carolyn Dugger on a winter night at Laurel Chapel Church near London, and they headed to the beach. They settled in Carrollton, Kentucky, where he started a teaching career. Exactly a year later in the fall of 1970, I completed my Bachelor of Science in Education. I quickly signed a teaching contract in Bullitt County. However, the London Draft Board nullified the contract and inducted me into the US Army. Off to Fort Knox I went. I went from "Joe College" to "G. I. Joe" in one week. I manipulated the ASVAB (Armed Services Vocational and Aptitude Test). They showed you a picture of a truck and asked, "Can you operate this?" I answered no. Screwdriver? No. Hammer? No. But when they showed me a typewriter, I answer *yes*. So they made me take the test again. "Most college graduates can operate a hammer!" the company commander screamed.

The second time around, I only fudged on some answers. If it was business-related or a health-related question, I answer *yes*. Bingo! After basic training, I got eight more weeks at Fort Knox (in my home state). I got "clerk school," where I amazed them with my 65 wpm skills. After that, I was sent for "medical training" at Fort Sam, Houston, Texas, for eight weeks. And after that, I lucked out and got sent to an army hospital. Moncrief Army Hospital, Fort Jackson, South Carolina, was where I would spend a year and a half. Dear God, I was Radar O'Reilly. It wasn't heaven, but it was not the hell some GIs experienced in Vietnam. I enrolled at University of South Carolina to get a student ID and free entry to Gamecock football games every other Saturday night at Williams Brice Stadium. I did pass the master's level courses, barely. Richard Nixon was president, and he too was sick of war. He declared that he wanted an *all-volunteer* army, and lets all of us who wanted an early *out* to have it. On February 14, 1972, after buying one of everything at the PX, I flew home to Lexington a civilian. Mom gave me the nicely decorated basement to live in. It's a simple brick three-bedroom on Tarleton Court. I was honest with her. I was twenty-three and going to sew a few wild oats for six months and then headed off to Western Kentucky University to get my master's degree. She smiled and said, "Welcome home, son." I bought a car with my army savings. I got drunk and crazy nightly. Connie fixed me up with a cute gal at the beauty shop. Life was grand. But came fall, I got my act back together and headed to Bowling Green.

Around the world in 1972: Eleven Israeli Olympians were murdered by Arabs. Mark Spitz won seven golds. Wrangler jeans were $12. Small pox was eradicated. There was civil war in Ireland. Alabama governor George Wallace was shot. The best films were *Poseidon* and *Deliverance*. Ben Affleck was born. UCLA won it all in 1970, 1971, and 1972. WKU made the final four and beat Kansas for third place.

1972–1973: My Wonderful Year at Western Kentucky University

In June of '72, I arrived at Western Kentucky University, a beautiful campus with twenty thousand happy students. I had been accepted into the master's program to study public school counseling, and I would earn a minor in public health. I moved into a tiny apartment at the foot of Henry Hardin Cherry Hall. I had a foldaway bed in a closet. It's a small apartment in an old house converted into six apartments for college students like myself. I loved it and the *freedom* that I had. The rent was around $175 a month. On weekends, college kids went to Barren River Reservoir, and we took a carload of girls with us. I was dating a cute girl from Tompkinsville who had a small apartment in the house next door. Before the fall semester rolled around, the university called me and invited me to an important meeting. The university needed a "teaching graduate assistant" to teach health courses and driver education courses. I accepted. I now had an office in the Tate Building and had my own driver education car for the year. My counseling department professors and classes were on the same floor. How convenient. By now, I was getting a nice VA check each month and a very nice check from WKU for teaching classes. This was the first time I really enjoyed college life. My students were very near my age, and a couple put the moves on me. To keep my job, I passed. By football season, I had met the girl who lived in the apartment next door to me. She was friendly, petite, smart, and looked great in her go-go boots. We attended football and basketball games and started spending a lot of time together. She too had grown up poor and on a tobacco farm. I still went to Nashville some weekends and listened to county live music at Tootsie's Orchid Lounge, shopped for records at the Ernest Tubb Store, which also had live music. Occasionally, when the Ryman Auditorium was not totally full, they would let college kids in free to fill up the back rows. I was watching the *Grand Ole Opry* for free. This was long before they built Opryland. Margie and I watched many basketball games at the historic Diddle Arena. We were in love. We planned a wedding for July 14, 1973. Her father, a minister, would marry us in his beautiful county church at twilight. She sewed her own wedding gown. That took talent. My family showed up for both my graduation and wedding. We both were graduated with teaching degrees, and by the end of the summer, we had decided on *Atlanta* as our future home. When you are in your seventies and look back in time and ask what would be your happiest year, for me, this would by my happiest year of all.

Around the world in 1973: Secretariat won the Triple Crown. The Sydney Opera House opened. Watergate hearings began. *Roe v. Wade* made abortion legal. The World Trade Center was built. The best movies were *Exorcist* and *The Sting*. The best entertainers were Abba, Dianna Ross, and Elton John. Popular TV shows were *The Waltons*, *M*A*S*H*, and *The Bob Newhart Show*. NCAA = UCLA, Oakland As beat the NY Mets in the 1973 World Series.

The Married Years

The Married Years

After working a couple of quick summer jobs to save up for the move to Atlanta, Margie and I loaded up our two cars and drove to Stone Mountain, Georgia, in DeKalb County, a suburb of Atlanta. We had a beautiful apartment overlooking the pool at Village Square. Margie worked briefly at Emory before her move to SW DeKalb High. I worked for six years as a physical education coordinator and guidance counselor at Rockbridge Elementary. I enjoyed my years at Rockbridge but knew this was a stepping-stone job. We enjoyed the things that a big city had to offer. We attended Atlanta Flames hockey games and Falcon and Braves games at Fulton County Stadium. The Neal Diamond concert played at the Fox, and fine dining at the House of Benihana were but a few of the many things we enjoyed. (Picture this: We were seated at a dark table inside Benihana Japanese Restaurant. The waitress brought a steaming plate to our table. The country boy came out in me. I said, "Wow, those are steaming hot rolls." Waitress whispered, "Not rolls . . . for *washy washy*!" That's right, I was about to dig into the hot towels. My wife never let me forget that one.) After four years, we purchased a beautiful new home in a subdivision where two other WKU couples lived. I attended the Peach Bowl, where Clemson and Baylor met. Margie and I attended Georgia versus Kentucky games. And on one hot fall afternoon, after the Georgia Bulldogs had soundly whipped our UK Wildcats in Athens, a Georgia fan yelled at us in the parking lot, "Go on back to Kentucky and stick to Kentucky Fried Chicken! We'll take care of the football!" I have hated the Dawgs ever since. Go, Tech! In 1977, our only child was born. I gave her a good Southern name, Mary Beth. She was a beautiful blue-eyed blonde and stole our hearts from day one. My mother and brother would come for visits and Uncle Ray and Aunt Judy as well. Bill and Ruth came down from Ohio. One year (1977) Ray gave me his NCAA Final Four tickets when UK did not advance that far. I watched Al McGuire win the national championship with his Marquette Warriors held at the Omni in Downtown Atlanta. We grew a small garden in our backyard each year and played in the sand at Myrtle Beach. We were pretty typical suburbanites.

Years passed. One day at work I noticed I was having chest pains. They continued, and I scheduled an appointment with our family doctor, Dr. Larry Ball. He performed a dozen tests and X-rays. I returned to his office a week later. "Mike," he said, "I have done every test I know to diagnose your chest pains, and I have found nothing physically wrong with you." We were puzzled. Then came the strangest question: "Are you happily married?"

After a long pause, I reply, "I am married, have a pretty wife, beautiful child, good job . . . but I cannot say I am happy *happy*."

He sent me to a doctor friend who diagnosed me with anxiety and prescribed a light dose of valium to end the chest pain. Years passed, and the chest pains returned. The doctor warned me that unresolved chest pain could lead to heart attacks in the late thirties. I changed jobs. I took a high school counseling job and dearly loved it. I looked back on other relatives who had had unhappy lives or marriages and *stuck* it out, and they were miserable. I spent a year mulling over what to do. The love that my wife and I had shared in those happy years at WKU and Atlanta as well was simply not there anymore. Was I cheating on her? No. Was she unfaithful to me? No. The doctor warned again that it was very dangerous to walk around with persistent chest pains. The most difficult decision in my life was facing me. What to do? What to do? To stop the chest pains, I took a path that made us all unhappy for a while: The divorce was final in 1980, and we parted. There were no words to describe the pain of hugging a little girl whom you worshiped goodbye. There was little comfort in knowing I would see her every other weekend. I had lived in a dysfunctional home and knew firsthand what that could do to people. I would not follow in my mother's footsteps. I changed everything in my life: my friends, my side of town, my church—everything. Eventually, the chest pains were gone. I was still young. I marched forward, not caring who won the NCAA, the final four, the World Series. There were no winners in *divorce*. I buried myself in my job.

Rockbridge Elem. 6 years
P.E. Teacher/Counselor
Stone Mountain Georgia

My New Condo in Atlanta McGill Park Downtown 1990

The '80s

In 1981, the State Department of Education selected me and four more counselors to work in the prestigious Governor's Honors Program. Each summer the top 600 high school students are selected to GHP by their high IQs, high test scores, and high GPAs. Nothing but the best are selected. In June, three hundred headed to North Georgia College, and the other three hundred headed South to Valdosta State University. It was a true honor to be nominated and selected to this august and talented *faculty*. This was one of the most interesting jobs I ever had. Working with gifted students and highly-talented students in music, art, and drama was so rewarding. These kids were your future doctors, representatives to Congress, professors, and governors. I cotaught a class in assertive training—how to get your point across without offending others. The students lived in one dorm, the faculty another. And yes, a few romances budded. We all had our meals at the university center. Summer nights in Valdosta were miserably hot. So I found a pub and had a beer. Out of nowhere, a brawl broke out. A guy my size knocked me upside the head. I fought back with all I had. He tore my fancy Izod shirt right off my back. For that, he must pay. I fought him all the way to the door before he split and ran. When the fight ended, I drove back to the faculty dorm with no shirt and a bloody nose. It's late, and folks were asleep. Thank you, Lord.

I spend the entire '80s and '90s working as a counselor at North Clayton Senior High, located a mile south of Hartsfield Jackson Airport-Atlanta. In the '80s, the school has a white student body, with a small group of blacks and Asians. I counsel the class of '82, '84, '86, and '88, all the way to graduation. I was in charge of testing, GHP, career day, four hundred students for scheduling and personal counseling. I coordinated the largest career day the county had ever seen; even the superintendent showed up. Most years I was in charge of graduation and baccalaureate. I attended every graduation from 1980 until 2001. The school system sent me to alcohol and drugs workshops, gave me educator tours to the Air Force Academy in Colorado and Naval Air Station in Norfolk. I was the guest of Johnson & Wales University in Providence, Rhode Island, for a week. They showed us colleges in the East, like Brown University, Boston College, and Harvard. I highly recommend these colleges to my best students. However, my seniors prefer Emory, University of Georgia, GT, West Georgia, and Georgia Southern. I sent so many students to the military; our local army recruiters gave me the state award for having the highest number of students entering the armed forces. I was an active member of GAE (Georgia Association of Educators), National Education Association, and GSCA (Georgia School Counselors Association), and I attend our annual meetings in Savannah.

Not all is rosy in school counseling. During my twenty-two-year career at NCHS, we had two students commit suicide and others were killed in car and bike wrecks. One senior (Barry Williams) gave his girlfriend a note in homeroom and then walked down to the gym with a small gun hidden in his coat. The girlfriend tipped off a coach who raced to the gym to find Barry. The gunshot went off just as the coach arrived. My job was to call the mother and tell her to come to the school as there was a problem. When she arrived at my office, I had the job of telling her the awful news. I just could not say he was dead. So I said, "Come with me in the ambulance, and we will go directly to the hospital ER."

The doctors pronounced Barry dead on arrival. I sent for his sister, a fifth grader at a nearby elementary school; his brother in tenth grade was already there. This would be the longest day of my counseling career. At the funeral, other counselors and I would stand by the casket to help bereaved students and family say goodbye to Barry.

Another student, Carlos Smith, had hanged himself a few years earlier while on Christmas break. We also lost Coach Moody, a young but obese assistant football coach. Andrea Eason, chairperson of the English Department, died of cancer. The school system opened up the Clayton County Crisis Team, and I took the lead position. There were seven high schools and dozens of other schools in the system. My job would be to drop whatever I was doing and go to the school that had a death or crisis. I was good at this and later trained counselors around the state in crisis intervention. One of my favorite former students was boarding a small plane for a skydiving adventure. While having his picture taken standing by the small plane, he backed up too far, and the propeller hit him and killed him instantly. There were highs and lows, and you never knew what a workday would hold in store for you. Years later, during the AIDS epidemic, a senior entered my office in tears. "Mr. Mosley," she said, "I have to drop out of school today."

"Why? We are so close to graduation."

She told me how her nineteen-year-old brother had advanced AIDS and her parents would not touch him and she must drop out and take care of him. I called AID Atlanta and asked for *help*. They sent people to her house to help them in every way they could. She graduated on time, and he passed away the next week. While classroom teaching is somewhat predictable, school counseling is not.

Around the world in 1982: Michael Jackson released "Thriller." The average rent in the United States was $320 a month. *E.T.* hit the theaters. *USA Today* was published. Russian President Brezhnev died of a heart attack. The top movies were *Poltergeist* and *On Golden Pond*. Popular TV shows were *Dynasty* and *Hill Street Blues*. Cardinals beat Milwaukee in the WS, and it's UNC over Georgetown, 63-62, in a thrilling NCAA Finals game. (Oops, in 1978, the UK Wildcats won the title).

By 1986, my whole world had changed, except for my job, which I love. I now lived in fashionable Buckhead, the nightclub of the South. Although I was pushing forty, I made sure it did not show. I even grew a full beard. I had a neighbor who was working on her DDS. Dr. Margaret Hopper was a great neighbor and friend. She gave me a lot of good advice. I went over to her place one day, and she had a dozen eggs sitting on the porch in the sun. I said, "Margaret, why the eggs on the porch?"

NORTH CLAYTON HIGH SCHOOL – COLLEGE PARK
MICHAEL D. MOSLEY, SENIOR CLASS
COUNSELOR
1990'S

My Daughter Mary Beth Graduates

"Well," she said, "the guy I was dating did me dirty, dropped me, and I saw him last night with another woman. Tonight, when he is dancing with her at Johnny's Hideaway, I plan to crack these rotten eggs on his new BMW."

It did not pay to cross this woman. I had lots of "bar buddies" by this time. I loved being single. I held Kentucky Derby parties, and the house was packed. John Travolta had nothing on me. I was the best disco dancer in Buckhead. Well, I thought so anyway. It was not unusual for me to dance at Limelight Lounge until 4:00 a.m. Their speakers were 6 feet tall and

6 feet wide. After a few rum and Cokes, you could find me on top of the speakers having a ball. These were some of the wildest times ever in Atlanta, and I was leading the pack. Everybody in town slept over at my place, except when my daughter came for weekends. I was Mr. High School Counselor on the south side of town, but I was blazing new trails on the north side. Living on the "wild side" will catch up with you eventually. The pillar of the community got a DUI, and I deserved it. At my court appearance, my attorney and I went into the judge's chambers, where I pulled out six $100 bills and gladly accepted the reduction to "reckless driving." I informed all my bar buddies, "I will not drink for *one calendar* year to prove to you all I am not a drunk." I did it too. After that, I slowed the pace of life a bit and started saving my money. I wanted a new *condo*. Relationships came and went. Many would date me for a few months and see that I was *not* the marrying kind, and they bailed on me. I deserved that too. The 1980s flew by. I was not sure what life had in store for me, I was having too much fun to care. Outside my wacky world, this was happening in 1988: A new car cost $10,400. The United States signed a nuclear treaty with the USSR. "Crack" showed up on American streets. The Winter Olympics kicked off in Calgary. The best films were *Rain Man* and *Die Hard*. The popular musical groups were U2 and Guns N' Roses. The Dodgers beat the Athletics in the WS, and the KU Jayhawks took home the 1988 NCAA title.

The '90s

The 1990s would be a slower lifestyle for me. I moved into a beautiful new condo near the heart of Atlanta called McGill Park. It was the city's attempt to bring white people back into the city. An old park was graded over, and new condos went up. I was one of the first to purchase, with the promise of "tax abatement." No taxes for seven years. Sweet deal.

My daughter was fifteen in 1992, and she brought her girlfriends downtown for sleepovers. Seeing Atlanta's skyline at night dazzled them. The Kentucky Derby Parties got so big, I had to move them to the clubhouse. By now, I had a dozen years of counseling experience, and I began to try new things at NCHS, which had transformed from a 96 percent white school to a 96 percent African American student body. I noticed that a lot of girls in the halls and cafeteria were expecting a baby. These were not wealthy families, so I did something that had never been done in counseling in that county. I set up a group called Already Parents and Parents to Be. The goal was to keep the girls (about ten) in high school, hold weekly group counseling sessions in the library so that the girls could get advice and benefit from what their peers had to share. They loved it, the school and county, not so much. When the word go out that it was a whopping success in preventing dropouts, Dr. Lovin, the superintendent, presented me with a beautiful award. A few years later, some of our best athletes said, "Not fair, you should set up a counseling group of some kind for us guys." The counselor at the elementary school nearby complained that she had some really troubled students. One had even set the teacher's hair on fire. I handpicked my five best male athletes and leaders in the junior class, and we paired them with the troubled third to fifth graders. One day a week they would go to the elementary school and work one on one with young boys. It worked. Their behavior improved. The county guidance director promptly responded with another beautiful award. I was proud of The Big Brothers Group.

Students would say to me, "Mr. Mosley, all the other good white teachers and counselors have moved to white schools. Will you leave us too?"

I gave the same answer many times: "Teenagers all do the same things, basically, black or white. I hated racism, and my mother had always taught us to get along with everybody. I would stay and finish out my career right here."

In 1994, I was proudly named the "Metro-Atlanta High School Counselor of the Year."

In 1995, I proudly watched my only child cross the stage. Mary Beth had graduated Rockdale County High School. I was proud of her, and like her parents, she enrolled at Georgia State and started work on a BS in Education.

Around the world in 1994: Tanya Harding whacked her competition in the Olympics. O. J. Simpson fled in the now famous "white bronco." Russia attacked Chechnya. The Clinton white water scandal began. The bullet train Eurostar traveled from London to Paris at 186 mph. Lisa Marie married Michael Jackson. The popular films were *Forest Gump*, *Pulp Fiction*, and *Shawshank Redemption*. Favorite TV shows were *Frasier*, *NYPD Blue*, and *The X-Files*. There was no World Series as players went on strike. Nolan Richards, well-known for his *40 Minutes of Hell*, coached the Arkansas Razorbacks to the 1994 NCAA Championship.

It was about this time that I decided to travel the world some. I now had a middle-class income, and if I shopped the trips, I could afford to travel to London, Paris, and beyond. I did a lot of group travel because it was affordable and somebody else had to do all the planning. I was off work every summer, and before long, I was a seasoned traveler, going to far-off places like Russia, Australia, and China. More about that later.

In 1996, the Games of Atlanta and the Summer Olympics, were coming to Atlanta, and I wanted to be a part of it somehow. I filled out a volunteer's application and asked for the basketball venue as that was the sport I loved most. I was assigned to the opening and closing ceremonies, and my job was to push a moving stage with Faith Hill, Gloria Estefan, Little Richard, and other stars all over the stadium floor. We also pushed large drum towers as well. We had eighty-five thousand present on opening night, and over 50 million TV viewers around the world. This was one the most rewarding experiences in my life. We spent many days practicing over and over to satisfy the demands of our LA producers. It was a smashing success. I could not have been prouder.

The year 2000 would be the saddest year of my life. I had just returned from a guided tour of Spain, Portugal, and Morocco, when my sister called and said, "If you want to see Mom alive, you need to come to Kentucky now." I visited her and spent time with her and came back to Atlanta. Two weeks later, she fell in her kitchen and passed away later that night at age seventy-four. This was the woman who had raised three kids on nurse aide pay. She was still the focal point in our lives, and now she was gone. When you are raised by a single parent and you lose that parent, you suffer twice as much. I went into a depression so deep a psychiatrist would later have to help me go forward with my life.

The 2000s

My Grandchildren

In 2001, finally, after thirty long years of teaching and counseling, my retirement year rolled around. I was only fifty-two years old on April 1, 2001, when it happened, but I took that retirement. The senior class of NCHS dedicated their annual to me. Coming from the students, that was quite an honor. Additionally, I was nominated and accepted into "Who's Who in American Education" in 2001. The last student to step into my office was quarterback D. J. Shockley, who went on to lead the Georgia Bulldogs to an SEC Championship a few years later. He made us all proud when he became a color commentator for ESPN in the early 2000s. At my retirement luncheon, I stood at the microphone in the school cafeteria and said farewell to the faculty and a job I had loved for twenty-two years. My brother and daughter were in the crowd. In a short speech, I said, "I will not miss freshmen girls fighting in the halls, chicken nuggets in the cafeteria, and the long drive through the downtown connector to get to work each day. I will miss this faculty." After some time off, the school system talked me into coming back and working "part time" a couple of years at an elementary school and one middle school. I continued to travel the world and became quite good at it. When 9/11 happened, I was all packed for a wild time at the beer gardens of Munich, Germany—Oktoberfest. That was canceled, of course.

In 2005, my daughter delivered a beautiful granddaughter, and we named her Mallory. I had never been a granddad before, so this was all new to me. I loved it. I did all I could to spoil her, and she quickly became the apple of my eye. I often reminded myself that Mallory was filling up that empty spot in my heart following the death of my mother. I'll admit I had really wanted a little grandson. And in just three years, a second grandchild was born. Prayers were answered; his name was Chase. When they were ages four and seven, I'd have them over for sleepovers. I loved taking them out to eat, having foot races in Piedmont Park, sitting on the floor at Barnes and Noble Bookstore and reading to them, and tucking them into bed a night. When God gives you retirement and grandkids and good health, you are about as blessed as you can be. I loved spending Christmas Eve with family again, something I had gotten totally away from and forgotten how wonderful those times can be.

Around the world in 2006: Saddam Hussein was sentenced to hang in Iraq. George W. Bush was president. Barry Bonds hit homerun 715 to pass the Babe. Temperatures in California hit 115 degrees and lingered for two weeks. Popular films were *Big Mama*, *Final Destination*, and *Superman Returns*. The best musical personalities were Beyonce, Bon Jovi, Mariah Carey, and Nine Inch Nails. The best TV shows were *Survivor*, *Bernie Mac Show*, and *Weakest Link*. In 2006, it's the Cards over the Tigers in the WS, and the University of Florida won the NCAA Basketball Tournament.

Around 2008, I accepted a teaching position with Georgia Highlands State College, part time. We have a home campus in Rome. In order to teach at the college level, you must have forty-five credit hours in your area (health) above the bachelor level. I had exactly that number, and in the spring semester, I became an assistant professor of health at the Cartersville campus. I have always loved teaching at the college/university level. No discipline problems, no faculty meetings. You simply drive onto campus and teach your classes and leave. Posting grades and even teaching classes were very high-tech and teacher-friendly. The curriculum was easy and fun to teach. We made sure our students got one final dose of sex education, nutrition, drug education, and others. My students were multicultural and came to class with the most interesting questions. Students who were majoring in nursing were my best students, and they raced through the course called Health Concepts. Occasionally, I would teach the easiest course the college had to offer, Walking for Fitness. After three years, I was moved to our Marietta campus at Southern Poly State University. Each semester, I required all students to do a ten-minute presentation on the health topic of their choice. One night, in my Marietta class, a young twenty-year-old student stepped in front of the class. Prior to this, the beautiful young lady had never spoken out in class. She said, "I am going to tell you about the night I 'overdosed' and 'died' but was brought back to life at Grady Memorial Hospital."

You could have heard a pin drop in the classroom. She was still going after twenty minutes, tears flowed as she spoke, and there was not a dry eye in the room. The follow-up discussion filled the room. Half the class had done drugs and at one time and had a scary time. Needless to say, she got an A+ for her open and heartfelt presentation. From that night forward, the class unloaded and told stories that curled my toes. When class was over, still they sat to hear the last word of the presenter. I invited a drug enforcement agent (DEA) to do a presentation in our class. A very bright well-dressed thirty-year-old agent showed up and talked for thirty minutes about the spread of drugs in the United States and what it had done to our country. Again, tears flowed as so many students had lost friends, relatives, and even parents to drugs. He told us how the war on drugs had failed and programs like "Just Say No" had been a disaster. A question-and-answer period followed his presentation. One of the students asked, "Where is the worst drug problem in America?"

"Well," he said, "you get on I-75 and go six hours north and you will be in the most drug-infested town in the US—London, Kentucky."

The class looked straight at me and giggled. With a red face and a look of astonishment, I told him that is my hometown. We had a chuckle. I had heard rumors about Southeast Kentucky, Ohio, and West Virginia, so I was not terribly shocked.

I taught two more years and enjoyed every minute of it. By this time, I had hit age sixty-two, was drawing Social Security, and no longer needed to work at all.

Around the world in 2010: A new house cost $232,800. The price of a loaf of bread increased to $2.49. The world's tallest building was the new 163-floor tower in Dubai. Space X launched *Dragon*. The Tea Party was born. Apple released the iPhone 4. Twenty-one miners died in a West Virginia coal mine collapse. President Obama signed the ACA Obamacare Bill. It's Giants over the Rangers in the WS, and Duke beat Butler in the 2010 NCAA Finals.

2011–2019

Year 2012 would be a great year for me. By now, my world travels had taken me to iconic destinations. I walked around the pyramids of Egypt, cruised on the Nile, saw the Sydney Opera House up close, had fallen in love in *Italia*, sipped vodka while cruising on the Neva River in Russia, walked in four Scandinavian countries, visited the house of Anne Frank in the Netherlands, sailed the straits of Gibraltar, stood on the Charles Bridge in Prague, slugged down ouzo in Greece, stood in the Hall of Mirrors in Versailles, sang old Irish tunes in the pubs of Dublin, traveled 186 mph from London to Paris, climbed into the Trojan Horse in Troy, drove 62 miles into Denali National Park, prayed in the house of the Holy Mother Mary in Ephesus, Turkey, and now *China*.

In 2012, I traveled to China, in Beijing and Shanghai. I walked the Great Wall of China for 2 miles. I know *not* why it was God's master plan that a simple boy who grew up on a farm in Kentucky would see thirty-six countries, but I am eternally grateful. I wanted to share my travel experiences with family, friends, and fellow world travelers. Write a book? That's it—write a book. And so I sat down at the computer, opened those travel albums one at a time, and began to write. It took me three months to write my book, *Memoirs of a World Traveler - 20 Years*. It took another three months working with Xlibris Publishing Company, and then at last, it arrived in my mailbox. I screamed in joy! It was beautiful and had captured my travels for over twenty years. I was so proud and still am of that book. And surprisingly, it did, in fact, sell a lot of copies. I wrote the last chapter from my hotel room in Shanghai, China, at age sixty-four. It sells at Amazon.com and Barnes and Noble. Check it out.

Other things were happening in 2012, and here they are: A gallon of gas cost $3.91. A movie ticket now cost $8.50. Queen Elizabeth II celebrated sixty years on the throne. A gunman slaughtered twelve in a theater in Aurora, Colorado. The Mars Rover landed on Mars. Pres. Barack Obama began his second term in office. Windows 8 was released. "I'll Have Another" won the Derby,

SF beat Detroit in the WS, and the Kentucky Wildcats beat the Kansas Jayhawks for the 2012 NCAA Championship, their eighth.

Year 2014 would be another banner year for me. I had always known that before I ended my world travels, I would do a Holy Land tour. It was a long, long flight to Israel, but I made in the spring. Tel Aviv was a modern city in every way. This was a nine-day group tour, and we headed north to Caesarea and on to the Sea of Galilee. Our group hopped aboard the "Jesus Boat," which had gospel music playing in the background. We stopped in the middle of the river, and the tour director talked about how Jesus had walked on this water and crossed it many times to see his friend Peter. You felt the closeness of God. Later that day, we ate at Peter's Restaurant, where tilapia, his favorite, was served. Although I had been baptized in 1974, I was first in line when they told us we were approaching the River Jordan and all those who wanted to be baptized right where John the Baptist baptized Jesus Christ should move forward. It was too good to be true. I put the white linen gown on and got in line. When the minister from our group actually lowered me into the water, I came out of the water without *sin*. It was one of the most moving moments in all my life. We moved on.

When you travel in Northern Israel, you are in Arab-held territory (Palestine). As our tour bus traveled south, we turned a corner, and a small boy standing in a field about 100 feet from us picked up a clod of dirt and hurled it at our bus. He knew that our bus was full of Americans as it passed his home each day. I thought to myself his act of hatred had been taught to him. We are not born with hatred for other religions or nationalities. The bus continued down to Jerusalem, and we walked inside the Cathedral of All Nations. Something happened here. Like many others, I worked my way to the altar and knelt to pray. And then it happened. Something out of this world touched me. It was warming. It was overwhelming. It was soul-filling. Tears flowed, and others saw the look on me and quickly moved to me. "What is it, Mike?"

If I told you the hand of God had touched me, you would think I was crazy. It happened. *It happened.* I walked a bit outside around the Garden of Gethsemane. I downplayed it, but my heart was swelling with pride that it had happened to me, a simple sinner. Later that day, I prayed a prayer of thanks at the Wailing Wall. We visited the place of the Last Supper, and then something happened that shocked me. The bus stopped, and our Jewish tour director stepped off the bus and shook hands with an Arab. He hopped aboard the bus and welcomed us back into Palestine. We stopped to eat, and they might have been Arabs, but they treated us like royalty. Our new TD would show us many holy places to include the dungeon and the place where Christ was laid after Crucifixion. I got on my knees and kissed that slab. A few days later, we arrived at the tomb of Jesus Christ. When you enter, you just want to fall on your knees and say, "Lord, I am not worthy to be in this holy place."

When the trip ended, I scolded myself for putting this trip off for so long. What was I thinking?

In 2015, by now, I had lived in my condo in Atlanta for sixteen years and even served as president of the board of directors of the homeowners association at Druid Forest Condos. I continued spending time with my grandkids, but they were growing into the preteen years, and I could see it coming. As a school counselor, I had this talk with parents many times. "As your child becomes a teenager, he longs for his 'grown-up ways,' pushes for more independence, and has little time for parents and even less for grandparents. Their friends, their cell phone, their band and athletic teams take all their time. They love their parents and grandparents but push them to the back." I would tell parents, "Don't fret, as they will come back to you at age twenty and twenty-one when they see you were not nearly as uncool as they thought."

I began taking lots of trips to Florida, and one night Carol and Eddie Reeder posted a picture of their home at Hawthorne at Leesburg on Facebook and invited me to visit sometime. I did visit and fell in love with the community. It would be mortgage-free, no water bill, taxes were $45 a year, and over fifty clubs and activities, like dragon-boat paddling on Lake Harris. I loved this place and started thinking of the move. Giving up my grandkids, brother, and daughter was difficult. But I was sixty-five years old, and the clock was ticking down. On December 30, 2014, I closed on my condo and headed to my new home in Central Florida. I love it here.

Around the world in 2015, these were happening: Caitlyn Jenner completed her transformation. Steve Harvey made huge Miss Universe mix-up. Gun deaths in America became common. Mexican immigrants began leaving. Same-sex marriages became legal. American Pharoh won the Derby, and Laurel Bridge won all the money at my Kentucky Derby Party. It's Royals over the Mets in the World Series, and Duke won its fifth NCAA.

The year 2016 would be the year of my fifty-year London High School reunion. I drove up to Kentucky and got a room at Hampton Inn - London and invited my sister Connie to join me. Sam Reeder also was in the hotel as well. I had not seen my classmates in forty years, so I did not recognize them all. When Steve Howard smiled, I knew it was him. We spent a wonderful afternoon watching the overhead flash-up pictures of our class of nearly one hundred people. I was proud of all my life accomplishments. We had lost around eleven of our classmates. Most all our teachers and principals had died. That part was sad. My old college classmate and roomie Bill York had passed, and I missed seeing him. The planning committee had done an amazing job.

The next day my sister and I drove all over Southeast Kentucky and visited the old cemeteries where all our relatives were laid to rest. Later we enjoyed good food at Daniel Boone Tavern and Inn in Berea, Kentucky. This was an election year, and out of nowhere, a longshot by the name of Donald Trump emerged. He had no political experience, had failed at almost everything he tried from Trump steaks, Trump university, Trump casinos, and he had paid no taxes for many years. By this time, the Republican Party was so unpopular that they had to invite the Tea Party extremists to the right to join them. They grew into a cancer on our nation. In November 2016, Trump loses the election but wins the electoral college. In the words of his own Secretary of State Rex Tillerson, "He's a fucking moron." More on this later.

Around the world in 2016, these were happening: The coup in Turkey failed. Britain voted to leave the EU. Russians caught interfering in US elections. Forty-nine died in mass shooting at an Orlando gay bar. The zika virus caused concern. Simone Biles dazzled the Rio Olympics. The Cubs won the World Series for the first time in 108 years, and the Villanova Wildcats took the 2016 NCAA title.

2020

Total calamity—2020 started off with the evening news telling of a deadly flu virus in China in January. Since we never trust any news coming out of China, many ignore the first warnings. By February, it had arrived in Washington State, and doctors said nothing was working to stop this virus. It was airborne. It was now inevitable that the whole country would soon have to deal with this deadly virus called corona virus and later Covid-19. The virus went straight to the lungs, replicated rapidly, and within days, the patients could not breathe. Emergency rooms were packed, and the ICU units filled just as fast. Italy was devastated, and so was Peru.

President Trump called it a *hoax*. By March, everything was shut down: restaurants, malls, schools, gyms, NCAA tournaments, the NBA. No part of the American life was unaffected. We had *no* vaccine. World Health Organization declared it a pandemic. Bottom line: It would kill millions. *We masked up!* But by the summer, two hundred thousand Americans got the virus and *died*. The death toll slowed a bit during the summer but picked back up again in the fall. Pfizer, AstraZeneca, Moderna, and Johnson & Johnson were working on vaccines, but nothing was coming out until December. I took my chances and went to California for a week. I never took the mask off, except to sleep. I spent time at Yosemite National Park, Muir Wood, and a long drive down the beach to Salenas, Monterey, and Pebble Beach. Delta Airlines had every seat blocked, and that helped some too. Anyway, I had a great time and came home covid-free. Unfortunately, my uncle Jack (seventy-seven), in Kentucky, got the virus and died three weeks later. No family escaped this dreadful disease. I wrote my VA doctor and asked for the first shot when it did become available. Luckily, I was the first in my family to get the Pfizer vaccine on December 22. What a great Christmas present! Two weeks later, I got the second dose. There was no NCAA Tournament because of the virus. Joe Biden beat Donald Trump in the November 3 election. Two democratic senate races were won by Democrats in Georgia, so the Senate would now be 50-50, and VP Kamala Harris would be breaking all ties.

On January 6, 2021, the unthinkable happened. As I told you earlier, the fringe of the Republican Party across America includes the Tea Party radicals. They hate blacks, Mexicans, Asians, gays, abortion, and all during last year's election, Donald Trump told them over and over that he could not lose the election. He made this claim before and after November 3rd. In fact, he has never conceded. This fed these all-white disenfranchised, marginalized, and poorly-educated zealots. Finally, it came to a head on Sunday, January 6, as Trump, in a morning rally speech, told them to go to the Capitol building and *fight*. They arrived with two bombs, guns, knives, and bear mace, and what started out as a protest grew into a riot and, finally, an *insurgency*. The nation's Capitol building was over taken. The Capitol police were quickly outnumbered, and it took four hours for help to come. Five people died that day. *Hatred*, pure and simple, was the underlying cause. Americans now had to stop and ask, how did we come to this? The answer is simple: racism. We have deep seeded racism in this country, and it's been simmering for decades. Unchecked racism over the decades has led to *inequality*. Millions of Americans no longer have faith that they can ever get to the "middle class." Affluent whites have stacked the deck so thoroughly, blacks and poor whites no longer have hope. Take hope away and you have lawlessness.

Not All White People Are Privileged.

If you read my autobiography, you can see that I grew up profoundly poor. I grew up in a dysfunctional home. I grew up with an alcoholic in the family. There was violence in our home. The money/income coming into our home put us at the "subsistence level," one step above outright poverty. We worked hard, but we never seemed to get ahead. Hope for a better life seemed beyond us. Blacks and Asians often think all white people live much better off than this, but there are millions of Americans who live like us—at the subsistence level.

Since the stock market crash of 2008, poor whites and poor blacks became poorer, worked longer hours, but still could not make enough to pay the rent, feed their families, go to the doctor when sick, so they became hopeless. When you feel hopeless, you do not do what the police officer says when he pulls you over. You feel you that you are not going to get a fair shake. You see, we are asking a part of our population to play by the rules, yet no matter what they do, they cannot win or get ahead. Their piece of the pie is denied. The result of this is some blacks refuse to play by "any rules," especially those of the white man. This must change.

In the 1990s (the Clinton years), the economy flourished, and as the old saying goes, "When the tide rises, *all* boats *rise*." Everybody did better in the 1990s, especially non-whites. They bought homes for the first time in our two-hundred-plus-year history. They could afford cars, health care, and they made advances that moved many of them into the middle class. Non-whites began to have *hope*. Race relations in the United States improved.

The great "bailout" of 2008 kept corporations from folding, but many took the money and gave it to executives of the company and reinvested the money in their own company's stocks. The *age of greed* began. The social advances we had made in the '90s were lost. In fact, millions of black Americans lost the only home they had ever owned. Once again, poor blacks and whites were feeling *hopeless*. Blacks begin to feel white people are "privileged" and the playing field is not even at all. During the marches held in major cities across America in 2020, the "Black Lives Matter" slogan emerged. The marches were justified, the rioting and looting, *unjustified*. Blacks took this slogan one step further; "WHITE PEOPLE ARE PRIVILEGED." My story shows this simply is not so. We do have people among us who are privileged, like the Trump family. Fred passed millions down to Donald J., and he passed it down to his children. But this is not *earned* privileges; it is bought privileges—big difference.

The great evil we are living with is *inequality*. Equal rights under the law is the way we are supposed to be living in this country. However, there is no equal housing for many, no equal labor/work for many, health care is not equally available, justice is not administered equally, even food and water are not even equally provided. Why is this? We live in a land of *great wealth*.

Let's look back at how I was able to break the shackles of poverty. First, you need strong encouragement to overcome obstacles. My uncles, grandmother, and mother all preached that *education* was the key, and they were right. I graduated high school. You would be amazed at the number of African Americans who fail to complete high school, and it is *free*. As a high school counselor at an all-black school, we'd have freshmen classes enter the door in the fall, and there would be 350 of them. By the end of the senior year and graduation, only 200 would be in a cap and gown. What happened to them? Where did they go? First of all, most black families have only the mother who is raising a large family. She leaves for work before the kids even get out of bed. I have called black parents at work and asked, "Why is your child not in school today?"

I'd get this answer: "Thank you for calling me, Mr. Mosley. I am on my way back to the house now. Bye."

Many black parents had great intentions but just not enough help. Some just did not push hard enough.

How did my brother get those first two college years paid for? He *earned* a scholarship and kept his grades up at all times. Also, Ted and I worked in factories in Indiana to pay for college. And yes, I had to go into the financial aid office and apply for scholarships (Methodist Scholarship), and when that ran out, I used the NDSL (National Defense Student Loan). My wife and I paid back student loans for around seven years after graduation. You see, where there is a *will*, there is a *way*. We are white people, but we sure as hell are *not privileged*.

How did I afford that masters at WKU? I made VA pay for it, and I worked for the university. I drove an old car and ate a lot of homemade pizza. My mother had always said, "Sacrifice for the future." Those were just words back then, but *now*, fifty years later, she was right. I saw college kids in my courses at Georgia Highlands College who were poorly dressed, drove junky cars, and sometimes they looked hungry, but I knew they too were "sacrificing for their future." Education, truly, is the key to beating poverty.

My sister graduated high school, finished cosmetology school, and at one time she owned the most prosperous beauty shop in Lexington. She pushed all four of her children to graduate high school, and they did. They too have degrees on the wall, proving, once and for all, "if you work hard, things will work out." My own daughter has a master's degree, and my grandkids are headed in the same direction. (Chase is an A student.) From generation to generation, we are passing down the idea that no matter what obstacles you put in front of us, "we will overcome."

"With Liberty and Justice and *Equality* for *All*"

Now comes the time in America when we truly must live up to our *creed*. We have adequate liberties. We have justice, but it is not equally applied. Our Congress is bought and paid for, and they put far too much pressure on the judicial branch to render their brand of justice. Common people are losing faith in this branch of government as well. It's time to bar the doors of Congress to special interests and the *rich*. It's also time for the wealthy to give a hand up, not a handout. The number of millionaires and billionaires in this country is staggering. The time has come for a wealth tax on the *very* rich. If you are not a millionaire, *relax*. I am not talking about you. It is time for corporations to pay a minimum tax. If you do business in the United States, and you make a great profit, be willing to pay taxes to pay for schools, fire and police departments. Pay your fair share for parks and recreation. Your tax money is needed to pay for the repairs of our bridges and the Eisenhower Interstate System. *You* use them, so help with the upkeep. Your share is not astronomical; it is based on your amount of yearly profit. You make a tiny profit, you pay a tiny tax. Poor people waited forty years for trickle-down economics to work—*it never worked, it never will.*

"We Hold These Truths to Be Self-Evident"

That all men are created equal. That's right—it's right there in the Declaration of Independence. Read it for yourself. Yet here we are in 2021, and who was the last group to get the covid *vaccine*? You guessed it, black and brown people. *Why?* Seems odd they would *not* want the vaccine as they were hit hardest. We have said for two hundred years, "We are a Christian nation based upon the Bible." (In reality, half the men who wrote the constitution, including good ole Thomas Jefferson, owned slaves.) It's time for us to bring that slogan (We are a Christian nation) out of the closet and be a little more Christian as in teaching the Ten Commandments in Sunday school. You'd be surprised how it sticks on kids.

CONCLUSION

In May, I will turn seventy-three years old. I have lived a long and joyful life. I live in an upper-middle-class home in Central Florida with a middle-class retirement income. God has blessed me with good health, children and grandchildren, travel around the world, and plenty food on the table. I am grateful. But I do not forget the difficult years, nor do I turn a blind eye to those who have much less than me. The injustice and inequality in this world eats at my very soul. I tell my brother, "It was God's intention that our first twenty years on this earth were very difficult so that these last twenty years (in retirement) can be appreciated."

One thing for sure, coming from a dysfunctional family helped me be a good school counselor. When kids would come into my office and say "Dad beat up my mom last night," I could relate. My brother and I have never, not once, laid a hand on a woman.

Last week, while on an all-day tour of the island of Oahu in Hawaii, I learned a lesson. We had a great tour director, and I tipped him well, but as I stepped off the bus, I whispered in his ear that he should avoid *politics* in his day-long monologue as it took away from an otherwise excellent presentation. After reading my last few pages, I see that I should follow my own advice. Politics is personal, and one's politics need not be shared with everyone. Forgive me. But those of us who have had the honor of seeing most every state, I am more in love with America than ever. And with all the issues we have here in the United States, it is still the greatest country in all the world. Now sing with me, "God bless the USA!"

Source: Pearson, Robert, "Thepeopleinformation," Free Internet information sources, Madison, Wisconsin.

World Travel

ABOUT THE AUTHOR

MICHAEL D. MOSLEY is a seventy-three-year old high school counselor and college professor (retired), who grew up in Kentucky, lived forty-two years of his life in Atlanta, Georgia, before spending the last six years in Leesburg, Florida. He holds a Bachelor of Science in Education, a master's degree in counseling and health, and a certificate in school administration. Mr. Mosley, who grew up on a tobacco farm in Kentucky, has finished a thirty-seven-year career in education. He is a proud father and grandfather. The author grew up very poor and worked his way through college. He has traveled to over thirty-five countries, forty-four states, and has authored a book on travel titled *Memoirs of a World Traveler - 20 Years* (Amazon.com or Barnes and Noble). This is Mr. Mosley's second book. He is an award-winning school counselor and teacher:

Member, Who's Who in American Education

Member, National Education Association

Member, Clayton County Education Association/Georgia School Counselor Association

Member, St. Marks United Methodist Church Peachtree Street, Atlanta

Honorary Member, Forest Park Rotary Club – Georgia

Author, *Memoirs of a World Traveler - 20 Years* - Amazon.com

Director of Guidance Award for Group Counseling Teen Girls

Principal's Award for Twenty-Two Years of Service to North Clayton High School

US Army Sharp Shooter Medal – M-16

1972 - US Army Commendation for Service to Moncrief Army Hospital

1975 - *Atlanta Journal* Recognition: Best Health and PE Program in Dekalb County

1989 - Superintendent's Award for "Big Brothers Group" at NCHS

1993 - Commanders Award for Highest Military Recruitment in Georgia

1994 - Metro-Atlanta High School Counselor of the Year

1996 - Letter of Commendation from Billy Payne - Olympic Games of 1996

2001 - Governor's Commendation for Service to the State of Georgia

2006 - President of the Druid Forest Condo Association - Atlanta

Printed in the United States
by Baker & Taylor Publisher Services